A Special Gift

for

from

A Family Keepsake

reflections from a
mother's heart

Your Life Story in
Your Own Words

THOMAS NELSON
Since 1798

NASHVILLE   DALLAS   MEXICO CITY   RIO DE JANEIRO   BEIJING

Published in Nashville, Tennessee, by Thomas Nelson. Thomas Nelson is a registered trademark of Thomas Nelson, Inc.

Thomas Nelson, Inc., titles may be purchased in bulk for educational, business, fund-raising, or sales promotional use. For information, please e-mail SpecialMarkets@ThomasNelson.com.

Designed by Koechel Peterson Design, Minneapolis, MN

ISBN-13: 978-1-4041-8774-0

Printed and bound in China

09 10 11 12 13 [RRD] 6 5 4 3 2 1

Contents

Introduction

DAYS PASS ...SEASONS CHANGE ... months meld into years, and we stand looking back at our lives—childhood memories, exciting moments, crises, and turning points.

In January, we think of new beginnings; in February, of Valentine's Day, first dates, and first kisses. Does ever a June pass without thoughts of our own wedding day? Surely summer evokes backseat memories of seemingly unending trips to grandma's house or the beach. And don't November and December bring to mind family traditions and celebrations cherished through the years?

Like ivy on the garden trellis, our lives are inescapably entwined with the seasons and months of the year. That is why we have designed this mother's memory journal in a twelve-month format. Each month features intriguing questions with space to write a personal answer. Questions explore family history, childhood memories, lighthearted incidents, cherished traditions, and the dreams and spiritual adventures encountered in a lifetime of living.

Whether you choose to complete the journal in a few days, a few weeks, or over the course of a year, the questions will take you on a journey through the times and seasons of your life. This creates a tangible family record to pass on as a gift to a son or daughter. It's a loving memoir of written words, opening a window into a mother's heart.

No matter what your age, memory and reminiscence open a richer, fuller understanding of who you are as a family. Let this memory journal be a starting point—a door into discussing and sharing the unique qualities of your life. May *Reflections from a Mother's Heart* draw you closer to each other as you share the experiences of a lifetime.

personal portrait

YOUR FULL GIVEN NAME ....

YOUR DATE OF BIRTH ....

YOUR PLACE OF BIRTH ....

YOUR MOTHER'S FULL NAME ....

    the place and date of her birth ....

....

YOUR FATHER'S FULL NAME ....

    the place and date of his birth ....

....

THE NAMES OF YOUR PATERNAL GRANDPARENTS ....

    the places and dates of their births ....

....

THE NAMES OF YOUR MATERNAL GRANDPARENTS ....

    the places and dates of their births ....

....

THE NAMES OF YOUR SIBLINGS ....

    the places and dates of their births ....

....

THE DATE AND PLACE OF YOUR MARRIAGE ....

THE FULL GIVEN NAME OF YOUR HUSBAND ....

THE NAMES AND BIRTH DATES OF YOUR CHILDREN ....

....

....

....

....

....

What Is Your Favorite . . . ?

FLOWER ....

PERFUME ....

COLOR ....

HYMN OR SONG ....

BOOK ....

AUTHOR ....

BIBLE VERSE ....

....

....

....

....

DESSERT ....

VACATION SPOT ....

TYPE OF FOOD ....

SPORT ....

MOVIE ....

LEISURE ACTIVITY ....

....

....

....

january

The beauty of the written word

is that it can be held

close to the heart

and read over and over again.

FLORENCE LITTAUER

WHO GAVE YOU YOUR NAME AND WHY?

....

....

....

....

....

....

....

....

....

....

....

....

....

....

....

....

....

....

DID YOU HAVE A NICKNAME?
How did you get it?

....
....
....
....
....
....
....
....
....
....
....
....
....
....
....
....
....
....
....
....
....
....
....
....
....
....
....

WHAT WAS YOUR FAVORITE PASTIME AS A CHILD?

....
....
....
....
....
....
....

Did you prefer playing alone or with someone else?

....
....
....
....
....
....
....

....
....
....
....
....

WHERE WAS YOUR CHILDHOOD HOME LOCATED?

....
....
....
....
....
....
....
....
....
....
....
....
....
....
....
....
....
....
....
....
....
....
....

Did you enjoy living there?

15

DESCRIBE YOUR
CHILDHOOD BEDROOM.

....
....
....
....
....
....
....
....
....
....
....
....
....
....
....
....
....
....
....
....
....
....
....
....
....
....

WHAT WAS THE VIEW
FROM YOUR WINDOW?

DESCRIBE WHAT THE FAMILY LIVING ROOM LOOKED LIKE WHEN YOU WERE A CHILD.

....
....
....
....
....
....
....
....

Where was your favorite place to sit?

....
....
....
....
....
....
....
....
....
....
....
....
....

WHAT DID YOUR FAMILY DO
IN THE EVENINGS?

WHERE DID YOUR FATHER GO TO WORK EVERY DAY?

What did he do?

HOW DID YOUR MOTHER SPEND HER DAY?

Did she have a job or do volunteer work outside the home?

....

....

....

....

....

....

....

....

....

....

....

....

....

....

....

....

....

....

....

....

....

....

....

....

DID YOU HAVE ANY
BROTHERS OR SISTERS?

How many, and what were their names?

....
....
....
....
....
....
....
....
....
....
....
....
....
....

*Tell about one
special memory
you have of
each sibling.*

....
....
....
....
....
....
....

SHARE A MEMORY OF YOUR GRANDPARENTS OR AN ELDERLY PERSON YOU LOVED.

Why were they so special to you?

WHAT CHILDHOOD MEMORY FIRST COMES TO MIND WHEN YOU THINK ABOUT WINTER?

....

....

....

....

....

....

....

....

....

....

....

....

....

....

....

....

....

....

....

....

....

....

february

For all of us,

today's experiences

are tomorrow's memories.

BARBARA JOHNSON

WERE YOU BAPTIZED OR DEDICATED?

If so, where and by whom?

When did you first go to church?

WHAT ARE YOUR EARLIEST MEMORIES OF CHURCH OR SUNDAY SCHOOL?

....

....

....

....

....

....

WHAT ....

CHURCH ....

DID YOU ....

ATTEND? ....

....

....

....

....

....

....

....

....

....

....

....

....

....

How did you view God when you were a child?

....
....
....
....
....
....
....
....
....
....
....
....
....
....
....
....
....
....
....

Did you say a prayer before you went to sleep?

WHO
TAUGHT
YOU HOW
TO PRAY?

WHO WAS THE FIRST PERSON
TO TALK TO YOU ABOUT GOD?

....
....
....
....
....
....
....
....
....
....
....
....

WHAT EFFECT
DID THIS HAVE
ON YOU?

....
....
....
....
....
....
....

WHEN DID YOU BECOME A CHRISTIAN?

How did your life change afterward?

Who gave you your first Bible,
and how old were you when you received it?

....
....
....
....
....

....

How did ....
it influence ....
your life? ....

....

....
....
....
....
....
....
....
....
....
....
....
....
....
....

HOW FAR DID YOU HAVE TO TRAVEL TO ATTEND ELEMENTARY, JUNIOR HIGH, AND HIGH SCHOOL?

How did you get there?

WHERE DID YOU GO TO ELEMENTARY SCHOOL?

....

....

....

Junior high?

....

....

....

....

High school?

....

....

....

....

....

....

What were your favorite subjects?

....

....

....

....

....

....

....

....

....

....

WHAT WAS ONE OF YOUR FAVORITE MEALS WHEN YOU WERE A CHILD?

Why was it your favorite?

....
....
....
....
....
....
....
....
....
....
....
....
....
....
....
....
....
....
....
....
....
....
....
....

DID YOU HAVE A FAVORITE PET?
What was its name?
Why was it your favorite?

....
....
....
....
....
....
....
....
....
....
....
....
....
....
....
....
....
....
....

WHAT CHORES DID YOU HAVE TO DO WHEN YOU WERE GROWING UP?

....

....

....

....

....

....

....

....

....

....

....

....

....

....

....

....

Did you get an allowance? How much was it?

....

....

....

....

WHAT WAS YOUR FIRST
PAYING JOB?

How much were you paid?

Do you have memories of a severe winter storm? What happened?

WHAT WERE YOUR FAVORITE WINTER ACTIVITIES AS A CHILD?

What do you enjoy about winter now?

WHEN DID YOU FIRST LEARN TO COOK?
Who taught you?

Tell about a memorable cooking moment.

....
....
....

Has your   ....
cooking   ....
changed   ....
over the   ....
years?   ....
....
....
....
....
....
....
....
....
....
....
....
....
....
....

DESCRIBE A MEMORABLE VALENTINE YOU RECEIVED.

SHARE YOUR FAVORITE DESSERT RECIPE FOR VALENTINE'S DAY.

....

....

....

....

....

....

....

....

....

....

....

....

Where did this recipe come from?

....

....

....

....

....

....

....

....

March

The mother's heart
is the child's schoolroom.

HENRY WARD BEECHER

DID THE PASTOR OR A VISITING MISSIONARY EVER COME TO YOUR HOUSE FOR DINNER OR TEA?

....

....

....

....

....

....

Share one vivid memory.

....

....

....

....

....

....

....

....

....

....

....

....

....

....

DID YOU EVER FEEL THAT GOD HAD A SPECIAL CALLING ON YOUR LIFE?

....

....

....

....

....

....

....

....

....

....

....

....

....

....

....

....

....

....

....

....

....

....

When did you first start to pray?

What do you remember about your early prayers?

DO YOU REMEMBER YOUR FIRST COMMUNION?

What influence did it have on you and your family?

WHO WAS YOUR
FAVORITE TEACHER?
Why?

....
....
....
....
....
....
....
....
....
....
....
....
....
....
....
....
....
....
....
....
....
....
....

DESCRIBE ONE OF YOUR FAVORITE CHILDHOOD DRESS-UP OUTFITS.

....
....
....
....
....
....
....
....
....
....
....
....

On what occasions would you wear it?

....
....
....
....
....
....
....
....
....
....
....

WHAT FASHIONS WERE POPULAR
WHEN YOU WERE IN HIGH SCHOOL?

Did you like them? Why or why not?

WHAT EXTRACURRICULAR ACTIVITIES WERE YOU INVOLVED IN DURING SCHOOL?

....

....

....

....

....

....

....

....

....

....

....

....

....

Why did you choose those activities?

....

....

....

....

....

....

....

....

....

WHAT CRAZY FADS DO YOU REMEMBER FROM SCHOOL?

....
....
....
....
....
....
....
....
....
....
....
....
....
....
....
....
....
....
....
....
....
....
....
....
....
....

MARCH

59

WHAT WAS ONE OF THE HARDEST THINGS YOU EVER HAD TO DO?

WHO WAS YOUR FIRST PUPPY LOVE?

....
....
....
....
....
....
....
....
....
....
....
....
....
....
....
....
....
....
....
....
....
....
....
....
....
....

WHEN DID YOU HAVE YOUR FIRST DATE?

Who was it with and what did you wear?
Where did you go?

....
....
....
....
....
....
....
....
....
....
....
....
....
....

What do you remember about your first kiss?

....
....
....
....
....
....

What did you do to celebrate birthdays
when you were growing up?

April

However time or circumstance
may come between a mother
and her child, their lives are
interwoven forever.

PAM BROWN

WHAT ARE SOME OF THE MOST MEMORABLE BOOKS YOU READ AS A CHILD?

WHAT MADE THEM MEMORABLE?

*What kinds
of books do
you enjoy
reading now?*

What were your family's finances like
when you were growing up?

....

....

....

....

....

....

....

....

....

....

....

....

How did that
affect you?

....

....

....

....

....

....

....

....

....

WHAT MISCHIEVOUS CHILDHOOD EXPERIENCE DO YOU REMEMBER?
Did your parents ever find out?

....
....
....
....
....
....
....
....
....
....
....
....
....
....
....
....
....
....
....
....

WHAT MEANINGFUL ADVICE DID YOU RECEIVE FROM AN ADULT?

....
....
....
....
....
....
....
....
....
....

What were the
circumstances?

....
....
....
....
....
....
....
....
....

As a teenager, did you rebel or do things your parents wouldn't have approved of?

....
....
....
....
....
....
....
....
....
....
....
....
....
....
....
....
....
....
....
....
....
....

How do you feel about that now?

WHAT ADVICE DO YOU HAVE FOR DATING?

....
....
....
....
....
....
....
....
....
....
....
....
....
....
....
....
....
....
....
....
....
....
....

WHAT THINGS DO YOU WISH YOU HAD DONE

in childhood or adolescence?

What are the things you are most glad you tried?

74

What things do you still hope
  to try someday?

DESCRIBE YOUR MOTHER IN HER BEST DRESS.

....
....
....
....
....
....
....
....
....
....

What smell (thing) reminds you most of your mother?

....
....
....
....
....
....
....
....
....
....
....
....
....
....

DESCRIBE YOUR FATHER IN HIS WORKING CLOTHES.

....

....

....

....

....

....

....

....

....

....

.... *What smell*

.... *(things)*

.... *remind you*

.... *most of your*

.... *father?*

....

....

....

....

....

....

....

....

Describe one particularly memorable event.

*Tell about a special outing you took with
your father or mother.*

WHAT WAS THE MOST TENDER DAY IN YOUR CHILDHOOD?

....
....
....
....
....
....
....
....
....
....
....
....
....
....
....
....
....
....
....
....
....
....
....
....
....
....

SHARE ONE OF YOUR MOTHER'S BEST RECIPES OR A RECIPE FOR ONE OF YOUR FAVORITE CHILDHOOD DISHES.

may

In search of my mother's garden,
I found my own.

ALICE WALKER

WHAT TOYS DID YOU LIKE TO PLAY WITH?

Why those particular toys?

....
....
....
....
....
....
....
....
....
....
....
....
....
....
....
....
....
....
....
....
....

....
....
....
....
....
....
....
....
....

Do you still have any of your childhood toys?

....
....
....
....
....
....
....
....
....
....
....
....

WHAT SCENT IMMEDIATELY
TAKES YOU BACK TO CHILDHOOD?

....
....
....
....
....
....

What sound
takes you
back?

....
....
....
....
....
....
....
....
....

Describe the
feelings they
evoke?

....
....
....
....
....
....

WHO WAS YOUR BEST
CHILDHOOD FRIEND?

Tell about one of your adventures together.

....
....
....
....
....
....
....
....
....
....
....
....
....
....
....
....
....
....

DID YOU EVER HAVE A SPECIAL HIDEAWAY OR PLAYHOUSE?

....

....

....

*What made
it special?*

....

....

....

....

....

....

....

....

....

....

....

....

....

....

....

....

....

*What responsibilities did your parents
require of you as a child? Explain how this
affected your growth and development.*

....
....
....
....
....
....
....
....
....
....
....
....
....
....
....
....
....
....
....
....
....

....

....

....

What were
some of   ....
the songs   ....
that were   ....
played?   ....
                   ....

....

....

....

....

....

....

....

....

....

....

....

....

....

WHAT KIND OF CAR DID YOUR FAMILY DRIVE?

....

....

....

....

.... *Were you*

.... *proud of it or*

.... *embarrassed*

.... *by it? Why?*

....

....

....

....

....

....

....

....

....

....

....

....

....

Did you attend any family reunions?
Share a memory of one.

....
....
....
....
....
....
....
....
....
....
....
....
....
....
....
....
....
....

Who was   ....
your most   ....
memorable   ....
relative?   ....

DID YOU GO TO CHURCH OR
COMMUNITY POTLUCKS?

How were they important to you and your family?

....
....
....
....
....
....
....
....
....
....
....
....
....
....
....
....
....
....
....

May

DID YOU GO TO COLLEGE OR TO A CAREER TRAINING SCHOOL?

Where did you go and why?

....
....
....
....
....
....
....
....
....
....
....
....
....
....
....

What was your major?

....
....
....
....

....
....
....

....

....

....

....

....

....

....

....

....

....

....

....

....

....

....

....

....

....

....

....

Where did you live when you were going to college or developing a career?

Describe an unforgettable experience from that time in your life.

WHAT WERE YOUR YOUTHFUL GOALS AND AMBITIONS FOR YOUR LIFE?

Which ones have you been able to fulfill?

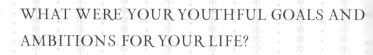

SHARE SOME INSIGHTS FROM SCRIPTURE THAT HAVE GUIDED YOUR SPIRITUAL JOURNEY.

Rings and jewels are not gifts,
but apologies for gifts. The only
gift is a portion of thyself.

RALPH WALDO EMERSON

june

HOW OLD WERE YOU WHEN YOU MET DAD, AND WHAT ATTRACTED YOU TO HIM?

....
....
....
....
....
....
....
....
....
....
....
....
....
....
....
....
....
....
....
....
....
....
....

What did you do on your
first date?

....
....
....
....
....
....
....
....
....
....
....
....

When did
you first
know you
wanted
to marry
him?

....
....
....
....
....
....
....
....

HOW DID HE PROPOSE TO YOU?

What day and year did you get married?

....
....
....
....
....
....
....
....
....
....
....
....
....
....

What city and church?

....
....
....
....
....
....

JUNE

....
....

103

WHAT DID YOUR WEDDING DRESS LOOK LIKE?

Did you have it made, or where did you buy it?

What was your wedding day like from beginning to end?

DID YOUR WEDDING CEREMONY INCLUDE A SPECIAL VOW THAT YOU BOTH WROTE TO EACH OTHER?

What was the significance of it?

....

....

....

....

....

....

....

....

....

....

....

....

....

....

....

....

....

....

....

....

....

....

....

Where did you go on your honeymoon?

....
....
....
....
....
....
....
....
....
....
....

Share one humorous incident.

....
....
....
....
....
....
....
....
....
....

WHAT WAS YOUR FIRST HOUSE OR APARTMENT TOGETHER LIKE?

....

....

....

....

....

....

....

....

....

....

....

....

....

....

....

....

*Do you
miss it?*

....

....

....

....

....

....

Do you remember one of the first meals you fixed after you were married?

What was it? Was it a success?

....

....

....

....

....

....

....

....

....

....

....

....

....

....

....

....

....

....

....

WHAT HAVE YOU LEARNED ABOUT
LOVE OVER THE YEARS?

....
....
....
....
....
....
....
....
....
....
....
....

What are some   ....
Scriptures that   ....
have guided you? ....

....

....
....
....
....
....

WHAT ADVICE WOULD YOU GIVE TO NEWLYWEDS?

WHAT DO YOU LOVE BEST ABOUT DAD NOW?

....

....

....

....

....

....

....

....

....

....

....

....

....

....

....

....

....

....

....

....

WHO WAS YOUR BEST FRIEND
AFTER YOU WERE MARRIED?
DESCRIBE SOME OF THE FUN
THINGS YOU DID TOGETHER.

....
....
....
....
....
....
....
....
....
....
....
....
....
....
....
....
....

I look back and see how I've

become who I am by a family

that found sweetness and joy

somewhere inside when . . .

life experience tasted bitter.

KATHY BOICE

july

SHARE A FAMILY TRADITION OR MEMORY FROM THE FOURTH OF JULY.

....
....
....
....
....
....
....
....
....
....
....
....
....
....
....
....
....
....
....
....
....
....
....
....
....

Have you ever participated in a rally
or demonstration?

....

....

....

What was
the cause?

....

....

....

....

....

What
were your
feelings
about it?

....

....

....

....

....

....

WHO IN YOUR FAMILY SERVED IN THE MILITARY AND WHEN?

....

....

....

....

....

....

....

....

....

....

....

....

....

....

Do you have
a special
memory of
that person?

....

....

....

....

....

....

WHEN AND HOW DID YOU LEARN TO SWIM?

....
....
....
....
....
....
....
....
....
....
....
....
....
....
....
....
....
....
....
....
....

DID YOU EVER GO CAMPING WITH YOUR FAMILY?

Where? Record one exceptional camping experience.

....
....
....
....
....
....
....

....
....
....
....
....
....
....
....
....
....
....
....
....
....

DID YOU GO TO SUMMER CAMP?

....
....

*Where
was it
located?*

*What
are some
special
memories
you have
from
there?*

....
....
....
....
....
....
....

DID YOU EVER PLANT A GARDEN WHILE GROWING UP?

....

....

....

....

....

What are some
gardening or
decorating tips
that you have
found helpful?

....

....

....

....

....

....

....

....

....

....

....

....

....

....

....

....

....

WHEN DID YOU TAKE YOUR FIRST TRIP BY PLANE, TRAIN, OR SHIP?

....
....
....
....
....
....
....
....
....
....
....
....
....
....
....
....
....
....
....
....

DID YOU EVER TRAVEL ABROAD?

....

....

....

How old were   ....
you and where   ....
did you go?   ....

....

....

....

....

....

....

....

Did you travel   ....
alone or with   ....
a group?   ....

....

....

....

....

....

....

DESCRIBE THE MOST FASCINATING PLACE YOU HAVE EVER VISITED.

....
....
....
....
....
....
....
....
....
....
....
....
....
....
....
....
....
....
....
....
....
....
....
....
....

TELL ABOUT A DRIVING TRIP WITH YOUR FAMILY.

What did you do in the car?

....
....
....
....
....
....
....
....
....
....
....
....
....
....
....
....
....
....
....
....
....
....
....

DID YOUR RELATIVES COME TO VISIT IN THE SUMMER OR DID YOU GO TO VISIT THEM?

What are some memories of those visits?

....

....

....

....

....

....

....

....

....

....

....

....

....

....

....

....

....

....

....

....

....

....

DID YOU SPEND SUMMER VACATIONS AT YOUR GRANDPARENTS' HOUSE?

....

....

....

....

Do you have any
special memories
of when you
stayed with them?

....

....

....

....

....

....

....

....

....

....

....

....

....

....

....

....

....

....
....
....
....
....
....
....
....
....
....
....
....
....
....
....
....
....
....
....
....
....
....
....

What are some travel tips or suggestions for a fun-filled vacation?

august

The family–

that dear octopus from whose tentacles

we never quite escape,

nor, in our inmost hearts, ever quite wish to.

DODIE SMITH

DID YOU LEARN TO PLAY A MUSICAL INSTRUMENT?

If so, tell about your memories of your music teacher, your lessons, and practice. If not, what instrument did you want to play and why?

Did you ever perform in a band, orchestra, or ensemble?

Who taught you to drive?

....
....
....
....
....
....
....
....
....
....
....
....

*What was
your first
car like?*

*Tell about
a funny or
frightening
driving
experience.*

....
....
....
....
....
....
....
....
....
....

DID A TRAGEDY EVER STRIKE YOUR FAMILY?

How were you affected?

Share a favorite poem or a passage of writing that has been especially meaningful in your life.

NAME A BOOK OR AUTHOR WHO HELPED YOU DEVELOP A PHILOSOPHY OF LIFE.

Share some of those insights.

....
....
....
....
....
....
....
....
....
....
....
....
....
....
....
....
....
....
....
....
....
....

DID YOU HAVE A COLLECTION WHEN YOU WERE GROWING UP?

....
....
....
....
....
....
....
....
....
....
....
....

What initially sparked your interest in it?

....
....
....
....
....
....
....
....
....

DESCRIBE A PERFECT SUMMER DAY.

WHAT KIND OF OUTDOOR WORK DO YOU ENJOY? HATE? WHY?

WHEN DID YOU LEARN HOW TO RIDE A BIKE,
or to water-ski, snow ski, roller-skate, or sail?

....

....

....

....

....

....

....

....

....

Share your
memories
of the
experiences.

....

....

....

....

....

....

....

....

....

....

WHAT SUMMER ACTIVITIES
DID YOUR FAMILY ENJOY?

DID YOU EVER MILK A COW OR SPEND TIME ON A FARM OR IN THE COUNTRY?

Share some of your memories.

DESCRIBE THE FIRST TRIP YOU TOOK ON YOUR OWN.

....
....
....
....
....
....
....
....
....

What places would you like to visit that you haven't already? Why?

....
....
....
....
....
....
....
....
....
....
....

DESCRIBE A FRIGHTENING OR DIFFICULT EXPERIENCE FROM CHILDHOOD.
How did you respond to it?

TELL ABOUT YOUR MOST UNFORGETTABLE SUMMER EXPERIENCE AS A CHILD.

september

Our lives are a mosaic of little things,

like putting a rose

in a vase on the table.

INGRID TROBISCH

How old were you when you really understood that God loves you?

Recall your early thoughts about God's love.

....
....
....
....
....
....
....
....
....
....
....
....
....
....
....
....
....
....
....

Describe a time in your life when you feel God led you in an unusual way.

....
....
....
....
....
....
....
....
....
....
....
....
....
....
....
....
....
....
....
....

HAVE YOU EVER VOLUNTEERED AT A CHURCH, CHARITY, OR ORGANIZATION? WHICH ONE?

Share any special memories you have from the experience.

....
....
....
....
....
....
....
....
....
....
....
....
....
....
....
....
....
....
....
....
....

If you could help any charity or organization, which one would you choose? Why?

WHAT SPECIAL TALENTS DID YOUR PARENTS NURTURE IN YOU?

....
....
....
....
....
....

How have you developed those talents over the years?

....
....
....
....

....
....
....
....
....
....
....
....
....
....
....

WHAT WOULD YOU STILL LIKE TO LEARN TO DO? WHY?

WHAT WOULD YOU DO DIFFERENTLY
IN LIFE IF YOU COULD?

WHAT DO YOU MOST WANT
OUT OF LIFE NOW?

....
....
....
....
....
....
....
....
....
....
....
....
....
....
....
....
....
....
....
....
....
....
....

DESCRIBE YOUR PERSONAL STYLE
in clothing, makeup
or skin care, and hair care.

....
....
....
....
....
....
....
....
....
....
....
....
....
....
....
....
....
....
....
....
....
....
....

DID YOU EVER LEARN TO SEW OR MAKE CRAFTS?
How and when?

....
....
....
....
....
....
....

*What was
the first thing
you made?*

....
....
....
....
....
....
....
....
....
....
....
....
....

SHARE SOME OF YOUR IDEAS ABOUT SUCCESSFUL ENTERTAINING.

....
....
....
....
....
....
....
....
....
....
....
....
....
....
....
....
....
....
....
....
....
....
....

HOW DO YOU MAKE
A HOUSE A HOME AND THE
PEOPLE IN IT FEEL LOVED?

october

How will our children know

who they are

if they don't know

where they came from?

Do you have any memories of harvesting a crop at a local farm?

....
....
....
....
....
....
....
....
....
....
....
....
....
....
....
....
....
....
....
....
....

DID YOU EVER CAN YOUR OWN VEGETABLES, JAMS, OR RELISHES?

DID YOU EVER GO ON A HAYRIDE OR BOB FOR APPLES?

Tell about any fun harvest activities you enjoyed with friends or family.

....

....

....

....

....

....

....

....

....

....

....

....

....

....

....

....

....

....

....

....

DID YOUR FAMILY EVER HAVE BACKYARD CAMPFIRES?

Did you roast marshmallows and sing songs?

DID YOU GO TRICK-OR-TREATING OR GO TO HARVEST PARTIES AT YOUR CHURCH?

What was your favorite costume you ever wore?

WHAT IS YOUR FAVORITE THING ABOUT FALL?

WHAT IS YOUR MOST VIVID FALL MEMORY?

....
....
....
....
....
....
....
....

What are the
sights and smells ....
of fall that you ....
enjoy most? ....
....
....
....
....
....
....
....

NAME YOUR FAVORITE HOBBY.
When and where did you start it?
Why do you enjoy it?

AS A TEENAGER, DID YOU BELONG TO A CLUB OR CHURCH YOUTH GROUP?

....

....

....

Tell about the individuals in the group who were most significant to you.

....

....

....

....

....

....

....

....

....

....

....

....

....

....

....

....

....

....

WHAT INDIVIDUALS HAVE HAD THE GREATEST IMPACT ON YOUR SPIRITUAL LIFE?

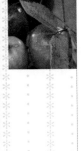

How did they impact your life?

DO YOU REMEMBER
WHEN YOU FOUND OUT
YOU WERE PREGNANT?

HOW DID YOU CHOOSE YOUR CHILDREN'S NAMES AND WHAT SIGNIFICANCE DO THEY HAVE FOR YOU?

WHAT IS ONE OF YOUR MOST CHERISHED MOMENTS AS A MOTHER?

....
....
....
....
....
....
....
....
....
....
....
....
....
....
....
....
....
....
....
....
....
....

What advice would you give to new mothers?

....
....
....
....
....
....
....
....
....
....
....
....
....
....
....
....
....
....
....
....
....
....

november

In our family an experience was not finished, nor truly experienced, unless written down or shared with another.

ANNE MORROW LINDBERGH

WHAT ARE YOUR
SPIRITUAL STRENGTHS?

....
....
....
....
....
....
....
....
....
....
....
....
....
....
....
....
....
....
....
....
....
....

Did you ever have
a spiritual mentor?

....
....
....
....
....
....
....
....
....
....
....
....
....
....
....
....
....
....
....
....
....
....
....

Have you
ever been a
mentor to
someone else?

HOW WOULD YOU LIKE TO GROW SPIRITUALLY?

WHO ARE SOME OF THE BEST SPEAKERS YOU HAVE EVER HEARD? WHY?

....
....
....
....
....
....
....

....

What did

....

you learn

....

from them?

....
....
....
....
....
....
....
....
....
....
....

HOW IS GOD'S WORD A PART OF YOUR LIFE?

....
....
....
....
....
....
....
....
....
....
....

What is your favorite Bible study you've ever done?

....
....
....
....
....
....
....

WHAT SPIRITUAL LEGACY WOULD YOU LIKE TO LEAVE FOR OTHERS?

....

....

....

....

....

....

Why is this
important
to you?

....

....

....

....

....

....

....

....

....

....

....

....

IS THERE A BIBLE VERSE
THAT PUZZLES YOU?
If so, which one and why?

Which verse blesses you the most? Why?

What verse do you turn to for comfort?

For strength?

185

WHAT BIBLE CHARACTER WOULD
YOU MOST LIKE TO MEET? WHY?

WHAT WERE SOME THANKSGIVING TRADITIONS IN YOUR FAMILY?

Did you have a favorite?

....
....
....
....
....
....
....
....
....
....
....
....
....
....
....
....
....
....

WHAT FAMILY CUSTOM WOULD YOU LIKE TO PASS ON TO YOUR CHILDREN AND GRANDCHILDREN?

SHARE A FAVORITE
THANKSGIVING RECIPE.

If everything special and warm and happy

in my formative years

could have been consolidated

into one word,

that word would have been Christmas.

GLORIA GAITHER

december

TELL ABOUT SOME CHRISTMAS
TRADITIONS IN YOUR FAMILY
and how you felt about them.

....

....

....

....

....

....

Were you ever in a Christmas program?

What role did you play?

....

....

....

....

....

....

....

....

....

....

....

How did you like the experience?

....

....

....

....

....

WHAT FAVORITE CHRISTMAS TREASURES HAVE YOU KEPT FROM YEAR TO YEAR?

Share their origins.

TELL ABOUT A MEMORABLE CHRISTMAS VISIT WITH RELATIVES.

WHAT IS YOUR FAVORITE CHRISTMAS CAROL? WHY?

*Did you have a Christmas stocking
or a special ornament when you were little?*

....
....
....
....
....
....

....

*What did it
look like?*

....
....
....

....
....
....
....
....
....
....
....
....
....
....
....
....

DESCRIBE THE CHRISTMAS THAT HAS BEEN THE MOST MEANINGFUL TO YOU.

....
....
....
....
....
....
....
....
....
....
....
....
....
....
....
....
....
....
....
....
....
....
....
....
....
....
....
....

....

....

....

....

....

....

....

....

....

....

....

....

....

....

....

....

....

....

....

....

....

....

*What is
the most
memorable
gift you
received when
you were
a child?*

*What was
the most
memorable
Christmas
you have had
with your
own children?*

TELL ABOUT A TIME WHEN GOD ANSWERED A SPECIFIC PRAYER.

WHAT ARE SOME THINGS
FROM YOUR CHILDHOOD THAT
YOU ARE THANKFUL FOR?

WHAT IS YOUR MOST TREASURED POSSESSION AND WHY?

WHAT WOULD YOU LIKE
TO SEE HAPPEN
IN THE NEXT TEN YEARS?

....
....
....
....
....
....
....
....
....
....
....
....
....

Why did you
choose those
things?

....
....
....
....
....
....
....
....
....
....

....

....

....

....

....

....

....

....

....

....

....

....

....

....

....

....

....

....

....

....

....

....

....

....

....

What has been the happiest time of your life?

WHAT WORD BEST DESCRIBES YOUR LIFE?
Explain why.

....

....

....

....

....

....

....

....

....

....

....

....

....

How would you like to be remembered?

....

....

....

....

....

....

....

....

....

WHAT ADVICE ABOUT LIFE DO YOU WANT OTHERS TO REMEMBER?

MY PRAYER FOR MY CHILDREN . . .